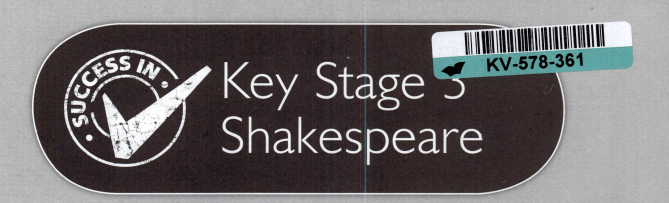

Key Stage 3 Shakespeare

KV-578-361

Scene-specific preparation for the
2008 national test

The Tempest

Contents

The story of *The Tempest*

1 Alonso, King of Naples and Antonio the usurper Duke of Milan, with their followers, are shipwrecked on their way back from the marriage of Alonso's daughter.

2 Prospero tells his daughter Miranda how they were driven out from his dukedom of Milan by his false brother Antonio and the King of Naples. Now, through his magical powers, Prospero has created the storm to right those wrongs.

3 Prospero checks what his spirit Ariel has done with the shipwrecked sailors, and then reminds Ariel of how he was rescued by Prospero from the witch Sycorax, mother of the creature Caliban.

4 Caliban, a monster-like creature, lusts after Miranda and resents Prospero for taking 'his' island from him.

5 Ferdinand, son of the King of Naples, follows Ariel's music until he meets Miranda. He is the first human she has met, and Prospero, when he realises that this is love at first sight, puts Ferdinand to the test.

6 Elsewhere on the island, the shipwrecked nobles, amazed at the freshness of their garments, wonder where they are, and lament the loss of Ferdinand.

7 Antonio encourages Sebastian to start plotting against Alonso, (as he had against Prospero) and they are stopped only by Ariel's magic.

8 Stephano and Trinculo, two of Alonso's shipwrecked servants, bump into Caliban, and introduce him to drink.

9 Ferdinand and Miranda fall in love, and Prospero accepts this.

10 Caliban encourages Stephano and Trinculo to kill Prospero.

11 Magical shapes, brought by Ariel, bring the evil nobles towards acknowledging their crimes, as Prospero planned.

12 Prospero gives Ferdinand Miranda's hand in marriage, and celebrates this with a magical pageant of goddesses who bless the couple.

13 Prospero remembers the conspiracy against him urged by Caliban, and uses Ariel's magic to distract and then torment the drunken three.

14 Prospero, now with all his enemies, past and present, in his power decides to forgive rather than to punish. He will give up the magic that has made possible the recognition and reconciliation that can now happen.

15 Prospero, having embraced Gonzalo, the one person who remained loyal to him, forgives Alonso and demands his dukedom back from his so-called brother, Antonio.

16 The innocence and purity of Ferdinand and Miranda signal a new beginning: the magic of the island has enabled the past crimes to be acknowledged and atoned for. Ariel's final task is to deal with Stephano, Trinculo and Caliban. Prospero no longer needs his magic, and we return from this on-stage island to the real world.

Set extracts – *The Tempest*

Extract 1: Act 3, Scene 2

Performance
They are arguing about what to drink. Stephano should gesture to Trinculo to be quiet as he says this

Performance
Trinculo should repeat these words in a sarcastic voice to show he thinks Stephano is trying to behave like a king

Performance
'Set' means Caliban should stare with his eyes fixed to show he is drunk

Language
'My' shows Stephano now thinks he owns Caliban like a possession

Character
Stephano is boasting saying he swam about 100 miles

Language
Kings often used to speak in French before Shakespeare's time, 'Monsieur' shows Stephano is trying to sound important and like a king

Theme
The dangers of poor leaders are shown by Caliban calling Stephano 'honour' as if he were a real king

---

Another part of the island.
Enter CALIBAN, STEPHANO, and TRINCULO.

STEPHANO
Tell not me! When the butt is out we will drink water – not a drop before. Therefore bear up, and board 'em. Servant-monster, drink to me.

TRINCULO
Servant-monster! The folly of this island! They say there's but five upon this isle; we are three of them. If the other two be brained like us, the state totters!

STEPHANO
Drink, servant-monster, when I bid thee! Thy eyes are almost set in thy head.

TRINCULO
Where should they be set else? He were a brave monster indeed, if they were set in his tail.

STEPHANO
My man-monster hath drowned his tongue in sack. For my part, the sea cannot drown me. I swam, ere I could recover the shore, five-and-thirty leagues off and on. By this light, thou shalt be my lieutenant, monster, or my standard.

TRINCULO
Your lieutenant, if you list: he's no standard.

STEPHANO
We'll not run, Monsieur Monster.

TRINCULO
Nor go neither – but you'll lie like dogs, and yet say nothing neither.

STEPHANO
Moon-calf, speak once in thy life, if thou beest a good moon-calf.

CALIBAN (*Very drunk*)
How does thy honour? Let me lick thy shoe. I'll not serve *him*. He is not valiant.

Character
Stephano is behaving like a ruler giving orders

Theme
The two extracts show what happens if leaders are foolish like Stephano and Trinculo – the state (the country) will totter (start collapsing)

Language
Trinculo makes a joke out of the word 'set'. He pretends to think Stephano means Caliban's eyes are placed in his head rather than staring

Language
Trinculo makes another joke by saying Caliban is not a standard (flagpole), he is too drunk to stand upright

Character
Caliban shows how he is prepared to worship the foolish Stephano in a demeaning (undignified) way. He will not serve Trinculo because he thinks he is a coward

Language/theme
The word 'lie' is used a lot in this scene, showing they can't trust each other

Theme
The idea of foolish leadership is continued here when Trinculo says 'Lord' in a sarcastic way

Language
'Natural' meaning innocent or fool shows that Trinculo thinks Caliban is foolish to call Stephano 'my lord'

Theme
The foolish leadership becomes even more comic with Caliban speaking so politely as he asks Stephano to listen to his idea ('suit' means a request or argument)

Performance
Ariel should stand behind Trinculo as he pretends to speak like him

Language
'Lie' and 'destroy thee' show how they are starting to fight and argue and not behave sensibly

TRINCULO
Thou liest, most ignorant monster! I am in case to jostle a constable. Why, thou debauched fish, thou, was there ever man a coward that hath drunk so much sack as I today? Wilt thou tell a monstrous lie, being but half a fish and half a monster?

CALIBAN
Lo, how he mocks me! Wilt thou let him, my lord?

TRINCULO
'Lord,' quoth he? That a monster should be such a natural!

CALIBAN
Lo, lo, again. Bite him to death, I prithee.

STEPHANO
Trinculo, keep a good tongue in your head. If you prove a mutineer – the next tree! The poor monster's my subject, and he shall not suffer indignity.

CALIBAN
I thank my noble lord. Wilt thou be pleased to hearken once again to the suit I made to thee?

STEPHANO
Marry, will I. Kneel and repeat it; I will stand, and so shall Trinculo.

Enter ARIEL (invisible)

CALIBAN
As told thee before, I am subject to a tyrant –
A sorcerer, that by his cunning hath cheated me
Of the island.

ARIEL
Thou liest.

CALIBAN (*To* TRINCULO)
'Thou liest,' thou jesting monkey, thou!
I would my valiant master would destroy thee!
I do not lie.

Performance
Trinculo should raise his fists to show Caliban he feels brave enough to fight a policeman

Character
Caliban starts to beg Stephano to tell off Trinculo. He is behaving like a child

Theme
Stephano is becoming like a dictator as he threatens to hang Trinculo

Character
Stephano is behaving like a king with lots of subjects when he only has two: Trinculo and Caliban

Performance
Stephano should gesture like a king to Caliban to make him kneel down

Theme
Caliban is now offering to become a subject to Stephano, who will be a worse ruler than Prospero

Performance
Trinculo should look upset and step away in a 'huff'

Theme
Caliban says Prospero used his magic power to capture the island

Character
Caliban shows his anger in these short harsh words ('from me he got it'). He feels he was supplanted like Prospero himself

Language
The use of this formal language 'compassed' instead of 'carried out' and 'the party' instead of saying 'him' shows Stephano sounding like a ruler

Performance
Ariel should stand behind Trinculo again to pretend he is speaking

Theme
'take his bottle from him' shows the three starting to behave like squabbling children

STEPHANO
Trinculo, if you trouble him any more in's tale, by this hand, I will <u>supplant</u> some of your teeth.

TRINCULO
<u>Why, I said nothing!</u>

STEPHANO
Mum, then, and no more. (*To* CALIBAN) Proceed.

CALIBAN
<u>I say, by sorcery he got this isle –</u>
<u>From me he got it</u>. If thy <u>greatness</u> will
Revenge it on him – for I know *thou* dar'st,
But <u>this thing</u> dare not –

STEPHANO
That's most certain.

CALIBAN
Thou shalt be lord of it, <u>and I'll serve thee.</u>

STEPHANO
How <u>now shall this be compassed? Canst thou bring me</u>
<u>to the party?</u>

CALIBAN
Yea, yea, my lord. I'll yield him thee asleep,
Where thou <u>may'st knock a nail into his head.</u>

ARIEL
<u>Thou liest: thou canst not.</u>

CALIBAN
What a pied ninny's this!
(*To* TRINCULO) <u>Thou scurvy patch!</u>
(*To* STEPHANO) I do <u>beseech</u> thy greatness, give him blows
<u>And take his bottle from him</u>. When that's gone,
He shall drink nought but brine – for I'll not show him
Where the quick freshes are.

STEPHANO
Trinculo, run into no further danger! Interrupt the monster one word further, and, by this hand, <u>I'll turn</u>
<u>my mercy out o' doors</u>, and make a stockfish of thee.

Character
Stephano is using complicated words as he acts like a ruler

Language
'Supplant' (replace) links what they are planning with the way Prospero was supplanted by his brother Antonio as Duke of Milan

Language
Caliban shows how he feels about Stephano by calling him 'thy greatness' and how he despises Trinculo by calling him 'this thing'

Theme/character
Although he wants to be free of Prospero's power, Caliban is foolishly willing to become Stephano's servant

Character
Caliban's bitter anger is clear in his violent idea for killing Prospero

Performance
Caliban should turn angrily to Trinculo then turn to Stephano and plead with him ('beseech')

Language/ character
Stephano sounds even more like a king able to give people mercy for their crimes

TRINCULO
Why, what did I? I did nothing. I'll go farther off.

Performance
Ariel should stand behind Trinculo and pretend to be Trinculo

Performance
Trinculo should sound hurt and upset and move away from the others

STEPHANO
Didst thou not say he lied?

ARIEL
Thou liest.

STEPHANO
Did I so? Take thou that! (*He hits* TRINCULO) As you like this, give me the lie another time!

Theme/ performance
Stephano should hit Trinculo. This shows the three continuing to fall out

Character
Trinculo shows his anger at Stephano and accuses him of being drunk

TRINCULO
I did not give the lie! Out o' your wits, and hearing too? A pox o' your bottle! This can sack and drinking do. A murrain on your monster, and the devil take your fingers!

Theme
The three have been drinking and drunkeness is not good for planning

Performance
Caliban should show his pleasure that Trinculo has been told off by laughing loudly

CALIBAN
Ha, ha, ha!

STEPHANO (*To* CALIBAN)
Now, forward with your tale.
(*To* TRINCULO) Prithee, stand farther off.

Performance
Trinculo should stand further and further away from the others, looking upset

CALIBAN
Beat him enough. After a little time, I'll beat him too.

Character
Caliban will only beat Trinculo when Stephano has done the same. He seems very fearful even of Trinculo

STEPHANO
(*To* TRINCULO) Stand farther! –
(*To* CALIBAN) Come, proceed.

CALIBAN
Why, as I told thee, 'tis a custom with him
I' th' afternoon to sleep. There thou mayst brain him,
Having first seized his books – or with a log
Batter his skull, or paunch him with a stake,
Or cut his wezand with thy knife. Remember
First to possess his books – for without them
He's but a sot, as I am, nor hath not
One spirit to command. They all do hate him
As rootedly as I. Burn but his books.
He has brave utensils – for so he calls them –
Which, when he has a house, he'll deck withal.
And that most deeply to consider is

Language
'Brain him', 'batter', 'paunch him' and 'cut' all show the violence Caliban is hoping will be used on Prospero

Theme
The repeated references to Prospero's books show the power of his magic

Character
Caliban shows his cleverness: first he tells Stephano it will be easy to kill Prospero because he will be sleeping, then he tempts Stephano by talking about the valuable things Prospero has and about Miranda's beauty

Language
The words 'beauty', 'nonpareil' (meaning without an equal) and 'far surpasseth' (much better than), all emphasise Miranda's beauty to tempt Stephano

Theme
The evil of their plot is emphasised: Miranda is expected to become Stephano's wife whether she wants to or not

Performance
Trinculo should say 'excellent' in a sarcastic way to show he is still upset, then Stephano should go over to him to apologise

Character
Caliban realises he will need to keep reminding drunken Stephano to keep his promise

Character
The thought that Prospero will be killed makes Caliban happy: he thinks he will be free

The beauty of his daughter. He himself
Calls her a nonpareil; I never saw a woman
But only Sycorax my dam and she –
But she as far surpasseth Sycorax,
As great'st does least.

STEPHANO
Is it so brave a lass?

CALIBAN
Ay, lord, she will become thy bed, I warrant,
and bring thee forth brave brood.

STEPHANO
Monster, I will kill this man. His daughter and I will be
king and queen – save our graces! – and Trinculo and
thyself shall be viceroys. Dost thou like the plot,
Trinculo?

TRINCULO
Excellent.

STEPHANO
Give me thy hand. I am sorry I beat thee: but while thou
liv'st, keep a good tongue in thy head.

CALIBAN
Within this half hour will he be asleep.
Wilt thou destroy him then?

STEPHANO
Ay, on mine honour!

ARIEL (*Aside*)
This will I tell my master.

CALIBAN
Thou mak'st me merry! I am full of pleasure.
Let us be jocund! Will you troll the catch
You taught me but while-ere?

STEPHANO
At thy request, monster, I will do reason, any reason. –
Come on, Trinculo, let us sing.

Character/performance
This speech shows that Caliban really appreciates beauty, like the speech about the music on the island later in this extract. He should say these lines in a gentle way

Performance
Stephano should show his interest in Miranda by emphasising 'brave' which means striking or wonderful

Character
Stephano shows his ambition by talking about being king

Language/Theme
Saying 'save our graces' sounds comic because Stephano is drunk and not at all fit to be a king

Language
The word 'honour' is false as Stephano is not going to act honourably in killing Prospero

Performance
Ariel says this to the audience so the others can't hear

Theme
Stephano's gracious granting of Caliban's request sounds comic, as if he is doing something important and not just offering to sing

Theme

The song is about freedom, which is what Caliban wants, though he is planning to serve Stephano

Character

Here and in the later speech Caliban shows he appreciates the beauty of music

Character/theme

Trinculo (unlike Stephano) shows his cowardice. The magic is shown as dangerous because they need to pray

Performance

Stephano is determined not to appear frightened, especially in front of his 'subject', Caliban

Theme

Caliban's speech shows the beauty of the island to be like a paradise. It links to Prospero's speech about the beautiful vision in the second extract

Theme/character

All Stephano can say is that music will be free, showing he is unable to appreciate beauty and will be a poor ruler

---

(*They sing*)
Flout 'em and scout 'em
And scout 'em and flout 'em;
Thought is free.

CALIBAN
That's not the tune.

ARIEL *plays the tune on a tabor and pipe.*

STEPHANO
What is this same?

TRINCULO
This is the tune of our catch, played by the picture of Nobody!

STEPHANO
If thou beest a man, show thyself in thy likeness! If thou beest a devil, take't as thou list.

TRINCULO
Oh, forgive me my sins!

STEPHANO
He that dies pays all debts. I defy thee! Mercy upon us!

CALIBAN
Art thou afeared?

STEPHANO
No, monster, not I.

CALIBAN
Be not afeard. The isle is full of noises,
Sounds and sweet airs, that give delight, and hurt not.
Sometimes a thousand twangling instruments
Will hum about mine ears – and sometimes voices,
That, if I then had waked after long sleep,
Will make me sleep again. And then, in dreaming,
The clouds methought would open, and show riches
Ready to drop upon me – that, when I waked,
I cried to dream again.

STEPHANO
This will prove a brave kingdom to me, where I shall have my music for nothing.

Language

The words of the song are about mocking and insulting, which makes them seem like squabbling children rather than plotting a murder

Performance

Stephano and Trinculo should look around them to try to see the musician

Language

'Devil', 'sin' and 'Mercy upon us' show how frightened they are, as they need to pray for forgiveness

Language

'Sweet', 'delight', 'hum' all describe how beautiful the music on the island can be

Character

Like the speech about Miranda being beautiful, this speech shows how Caliban appreciates beauty

CALIBAN

When Prospero is destroyed.

Language
'By and by', means 'not now', showing Stephano putting off the murder

STEPHANO

That shall be by and by. I remember the story.

Character
Caliban has seen how easily Stephano can be distracted, so he makes sure to remind Stephano he must do the murder

TRINCULO

The sound is going away. Let's follow it, and after do our work.

Theme
Following the sound shows that they will make poor rulers because they are so easily distracted

STEPHANO

Lead, monster. We'll follow. I would I could see this taborer: he lays it on.

Performance
Trinculo should look excited as he follows the sound

TRINCULO

Wilt come? I'll follow, Stephano.

Exeunt.

Extract 2: Act 4, Scene 1, lines 139 to 262

Character/ performance
Prospero should look angry and gesture as he suddenly remembers the plot and dismisses the spirits

PROSPERO (*Aside*)
I had forgot that foul conspiracy
Of the beast Caliban and his confederates
Against my life! The minute of their plot
Is almost come.
(*To the Spirits*) Well done! avoid. No more!

Language
'Foul conspiracy' and 'beast' show the anger Prospero feels towards Caliban

FERDINAND
This is strange. Your father's in some passion
That works him strongly.

Performance
Prospero should behave in an agitated way which Ferdinand notices

MIRANDA
Never till this day
Saw I him touched with anger, so distempered.

Theme
'Against my life' emphasises the evil of Caliban's plot and links it with Antonio and Sebastian plotting to kill the king

Character
Miranda's comment shows how unusual it is for Prospero to be so upset

PROSPERO
You do look, my son, in a moved sort,
As if you were dismayed. Be cheerful, sir.
Our revels now are ended. These our actors,
As I foretold you, were all spirits – and
Are melted into air, into thin air.
And, like the baseless fabric of this vision,
The cloud-capped towers, the gorgeous palaces,
The solemn temples, the great globe itself,

Performance
Ferdinand should look anxious at Prospero's behaviour

Language
'cloud-capped', 'gorgeous', 'solemn' and 'great' all emphasise the magnificence of the whole world. The references to the actors and to the globe remind the audience that they are in the world of the theatre

Theme
Like the storm, the vision they have been watching was created by Prospero's magic and has now disappeared

Theme

All the people who will live in the world will disappear, all power is temporary as we all die: 'our little life is rounded with a sleep'

Performance

Prospero should continue to look anxious and walk around the stage

Language

'With a thought' means as quick as thinking showing the power of the magic, things happen instantly

Character

Ariel knows he will soon be free and is willingly carrying out all Prospero's thoughts. He calls Prospero his 'commander', showing how obedient he is being

Theme

Ariel's description of the drunken Caliban, Stephano and Trinculo trying to hit the air and beating the ground is ridiculous and shows they are unfit to rule the island. It links to the first extract

---

Yea, all which it inherit, shall dissolve,
And, like this insubstantial pageant faded,
Leave not a rack behind. We are such stuff
As dreams are made on; and our little life
Is rounded with a sleep. Sir, I am vexed.
Bear with my weakness: my old brain is troubled.
Be not disturbed with my infirmity.
If you be pleased, retire into my cell,
And there repose. A turn or two I'll walk,
To still my beating mind.

FERDINAND and MIRANDA
We wish your peace.

Exit MIRANDA, *with* FERDINAND

PROSPERO (*Calling* ARIEL)
Come with a thought!
(*To* FERDINAND *and* MIRANDA) I thank thee. Ariel, come!

Enter ARIEL.

ARIEL
Thy thoughts I cleave to. What's thy pleasure?

PROSPERO
Spirit,
We must prepare to meet with Caliban.

ARIEL
Ay, my commander. When I presented Ceres,
I thought to have told thee of it – but I feared
Lest I might anger thee.

PROSPERO
Say again, where didst thou leave these varlets?

ARIEL
I told you, sir, they were red-hot with drinking –
So full of valour that they smote the air
For breathing in their faces; beat the ground
For kissing of their feet – yet always bending
Towards their project. Then I beat my tabor:
At which, like unbacked colts they pricked their ears,
Advanced their eyelids, lifted up their noses
As they smelt music; so I charmed their ears,

Language

'Dissolve', 'faded', 'leave not a rack (nothing) behind' all emphasise that life is temporary

Character

'Weakness' and 'old brain' show that Prospero is feeling his age and nearly forgot that Caliban is planning to kill him

Performance

Ariel should behave obediently towards Prospero

Character/ language

'Feared lest I might anger thee' shows how Ariel wants to please Prospero

Language

'Varlets' means rogues, emphasising they are evil

Language

'Unbacked (untrained) colts' and 'lifted up their noses' makes the three plotters seem like animals, easily led and not sensible enough to be rulers

Character/language
They were like calves following a cow, showing again how easily they are led

Theme
The slimy pool Ariel leaves them in contrasts with Caliban's beautiful description of the island in the first extract. Their evil means they deserve to be in the filthy pool

Language
'Stale' means bait which emphasises they are like animals caught by bait

Language
'Cankers' means becomes corrupted showing how Caliban is becoming more evil

Performance
Ariel hangs up all the clothes

Character
Caliban is still trying to keep Stephano and Trinculo quiet so they can creep up and kill Prospero

Theme
Talking about 'horse-piss' is comic and shows they are not really thinking about the serious business of murder

---

That, calf-like, they my lowing followed, through
Toothed briers, sharp furzes, pricking gorse and thorns,
Which entered their frail shins. At last I left them
I'the filthy-mantled pool beyond your cell,
There dancing up to the chins, that the foul lake
O'erstunk their feet.

PROSPERO
This was well done, my bird!
Thy shape invisible retain thou still.
The trumpery in my house, go bring it hither,
For stale to catch these thieves.

ARIEL
I go, I go.

Exit.

PROSPERO
A devil, a born devil, on whose nature
Nurture can never stick – on whom my pains,
Humanely taken, all, all lost, quite lost!
And as with age his body uglier grows,
So his mind cankers. I will plague them all,
Even to roaring.

Re-enter ARIEL, with a load of flashy, shining clothing.
Come, hang them on this line.

Enter CALIBAN, STEPHANO and TRINCULO, soaked and dirty. (ARIEL and PROSPERO are invisible to them.)

CALIBAN
Pray you, tread softly, that the blind mole may not
Hear a foot fall. We now are near his cell.

STEPHANO
Monster, your fairy, which you say is a harmless fairy, has done little better than played the Jack with us.

TRINCULO
Monster, I do smell all horse-piss – at which my nose is in great indignation.

Language
'Toothed', 'sharp', 'pricking' and 'thorns' all show the unpleasant and painful parts of the island Ariel has led them through

Performance
As he describes what happened to them Ariel should show through his actions how they were being stung and pricked by the plants

Theme/character
All Prospero's efforts to educate and civilise Caliban have been wasted. Prospero is very disappointed. This is emphasised by 'lost' being repeated

Performance
Prospero should show his anger by saying 'plague them all' and 'roaring' really fiercely

Character
As in the first extract Stephano and Trinculo are easily distracted and want to talk about what tricks Ariel has played on them rather than concentrate on the murder plot

Performance
Both Stephano and Trinculo should look angry and shake their fists at Caliban

Language
'My lord' shows how Caliban is trying to be nice to Stephano so that he will carry out the murder

Performance
Caliban should whisper when he says 'speak softly'. Trinculo should speak loudly to show they are ignoring Caliban

Character
Stephano is so determined to get back the bottle that he will risk drowning. He and Trinculo are more interested in drink than the plot to murder Prospero

Language
'Foot-licker' shows how far Caliban will go to serve Stephano: he will become Stephano's slave

STEPHANO
So is mine. Do you hear, monster? If I should take a displeasure against <u>you, look you</u> –

TRINCULO
Thou wert but a <u>lost monster</u>.

CALIBAN
<u>Good my lord, give me thy favour still.</u>
Be patient, <u>for the prize I'll bring thee to</u>
Shall <u>hoodwink this mischance. Therefore speak softly;</u>
<u>All's hushed as midnight yet.</u>

TRINCULO
Ay, <u>but to lose</u> our bottles in the pool!

STEPHANO
<u>There</u> is not only <u>disgrace</u> and <u>dishonour</u> in that, monster, but an <u>infinite loss</u>.

TRINCULO
That's more to me than my wetting. Yet this is your harmless fairy, monster.

STEPHANO
I <u>will fetch off my</u> bottle, though I be <u>o'er ears for</u> my labour.

CALIBAN
Prithee, <u>my King, be quiet.</u> Seest thou here:
This is the mouth o' the cell. No noise, and enter.
Do that good mischief which may make this island
Thine own for ever, and I, thy Caliban,
For aye <u>thy foot-licker.</u>

STEPHANO
<u>Give me thy hand; I do begin to have bloody thoughts.</u>

TRINCULO
O King Stephano! O peer! O worthy Stephano!
<u>Look</u> what <u>wardrobe here is for thee!</u>

CALIBAN
Let it alone, thou fool! <u>It is but trash.</u>

Character
They are now threatening to punish Caliban because of what has happened to them. In the first extract it was Trinculo who was threatened

Character
To try to make them concentrate, Caliban cleverly reminds them that ruling the island will be their prize for the murder

Language/theme
'Disgrace', 'dishonour' and 'infinite loss' are serious ideas but Stephano is using them to talk about losing their drink, which makes them seem ridiculous and comic

Performance
Caliban should whisper when he says these lines and try to make Stephano and Trinculo be quiet

Language/ character
As in the first extract, Stephano uses the language of a king when he thinks of taking over the island

Performance
Trinculo should rush excitedly to the clothes when he sees them and Caliban should look angry and try to drag Trinculo away

TRINCULO
O, ho, monster! We know what belongs to a frippery. O King Stephano!

They take and try on the clothes that ARIEL has left.

STEPHANO
Put off that gown, Trinculo. By this hand, I'll have that gown!

TRINCULO
Thy grace shall have it.

CALIBAN
The dropsy drown this fool! What do you mean
To dote thus on such luggage? Let's alone
And do the murder first! If he awake,
From toe to crown he'll fill our skins with pinches,
Make *us* strange stuff.

STEPHANO
Be you quiet, monster. Mistress line, is not this my jerkin? Now is the jerkin under the line: now, jerkin, you are like to lose your hair, and prove a bald jerkin.

TRINCULO
Do, do! We steal by line and level, an it like your grace.

STEPHANO
I thank thee for that jest: here's a garment for it. Wit shall not go unrewarded while I am king of this country. 'Steal by line and level' is an excellent pass of pate! There's another garment for it.

TRINCULO
Monster, come put some lime upon your fingers, and away with the rest.

CALIBAN
I will have none on't! We shall lose our time,
And all be turned to barnacles, or to apes
With foreheads villainous low.

STEPHANO
Monster, lay-to your fingers! Help to bear this away where my hogshead of wine is, or I'll turn you out of my kingdom. Go to, carry this!

TRINCULO
And this!

STEPHANO
Ay, and this.

*A sudden noise of hunting-horns and dogs. Enter Spirits, in
the form of large hunting-dogs. They chase STEPHANO,
TRINCULO, and CALIBAN to and fro, with ARIEL and
PROSPERO shouting to urge them on.*

PROSPERO
Hey, Mountain, hey!

ARIEL
Silver! There it goes, Silver!

PROSPERO
Fury, Fury! There, Tyrant, there! Hark, hark!

*CALIBAN, STEPHANO, and TRINCULO are chased
away.*

Go, charge my goblins that they grind their joints
With dry convulsions; shorten up their sinews
With aged cramps – and more pinch-spotted make them
Than pard or cat-o'-mountain.

ARIEL
Hark, they roar!

PROSPERO
Let them be hunted soundly. At this hour
Lies at my mercy all mine enemies.
Shortly shall all my labours end, and thou
Shalt have the air at freedom. For a little
Follow, and do me service.

Exeunt.

Focus on character

Highlight the key words in the table below and fill in the blank rows with your own points, quotations and personal responses.

Extract 1: Act 3, Scene 3

Points	Quotations	Personal responses
Stephano Stephano is a drunkard who enjoys it when Caliban treats him as a king. He bullies and beats Trinculo, but still sees him as a friend who is his inferior.	*Stephano: The poor monster's my subject,…* *… by this hand, I will supplant some of your teeth…*	Stephano's drinking and boasting, his threats to Trinculo and his vulgar behaviour show how unlike a true king he is.
Stephano is easily fooled, by drink and by magic, but he is not a coward, and he reacts defiantly to hearing Ariel's music. He is ready to murder to become king of the island.	*Monster, I will kill this man; his daughter and I will be king and queen – save our graces!*	Stephano has none of the qualities a ruler needs. He could never deserve Miranda, and Prospero is truly king-like by comparison. Prospero has magical power – Stephano just thinks he has it because of the drink.
Trinculo Trinculo is a follower, not a leader, but he has more brains than Stephano. He is (slightly) less drunk, and thinks Caliban seems foolish in his praise for Stephano. He is jealous of Caliban's influence with Stephano and resents being beaten for nothing. He is terrified by Ariel's music.	*Trinculo: The folly of this island!* *…thou debauched fish, thou,…* **or** *That a monster should be such a natural!* **or** *A pox o' your bottle!* *O, forgive me my sins!*	The exchanges between Stephano and Trinculo are partly to amuse the audience. They are two Elizabethan Londoners dumped on a magic island. It is Trinculo who uses the language of good and evil when he is frightened.
Caliban Caliban gets drunk easily and this makes him a figure of fun at first. He has contempt for Trinculo, and is jealous of him, but treats Stephano as a king.	*Caliban: How does thy honour? Let me lick thy shoe; I'll not serve* **him.** *He is not valiant.* **or** *… Bite him to death, I prithee.* *… my noble lord…*	Like the people of newly-conquered colonies in Shakespeare's time, Caliban falls victim to drink. Caliban's savagery shows first in his threats to Trinculo. He does not seem to want to be a ruler himself, but to serve Stephano.
Caliban feels that Prospero 'cheated me of the island'. He may be drunk but still knows that Prospero's power is in his books. He is cunning enough to tempt Stephano with Miranda's beauty because he wants him to replace Prospero as lord of the island.	*… I am subject to a tyrant, a sorcerer…* *…thou may'st knock a nail into his head…* *Batter his skull, or paunch him with a stake,* *Or cut his wezand with thy knife… they all do hate him* *As rootedly as I. Burn but his books…* *…that most deeply to consider is* *The beauty of his daughter… she will become thy bed, I warrant,…*	The violence of his language in suggesting ways of killing Prospero is startlingly savage and full of resentful hatred. He tempts Stephano with sex as well as with the prospect of power. Of the three, he is the one who is most determined to destroy Prospero and the audience will pick up that there is real danger in his fierce feelings of resentment.

Focus on character

Highlight the key words in the table below and fill in the blank rows with your own points, quotations and personal responses.

Extract 2: Act 4, Scene 1, lines 139 to 262

Points	Quotations	Personal responses
Stephano Stephano appears filthy and pathetic – no real threat to anyone since he thinks that losing his bottle is 'an infinite loss' and he is so concerned with appearances that he competes with Trinculo for a particular gown.	*Stephano: By this hand, I'll have that gown!* **or** *I thank thee for that jest; here's a garment for't; wit shall not go unrewarded while I am king of this country.*	Prospero's reference to the 'foul conspiracy / Of the beast Caliban and his confederates' reminds the audience that their 'project' is to kill him. However when Stephano and Trinculo squabble over a gown we know that their concern for appearances will be their downfall. The real focus of the play at this point is on Prospero's inner conflict rather than with the 'conspiracy'.
Trinculo Trinculo was the more sensible earlier on, but now he is duped by the 'trumpery' and has taken on Caliban's language of 'King Stephano'.	*Trinculo: Monster, I do smell all horse-piss…* *O King Stephano! O peer! O worthy Stephano! Look what wardrobe here is for thee!*	Trinculo has lost his earlier sense of what is real and what is not. He is as excited as Stephano by the 'trumpery' that Prospero knew would distract them from their murderous intentions.
Caliban Only Caliban is firm in his purpose to kill Prospero. He (unlike the others) is not fooled by the 'luggage' on display to distract them.	*Caliban: What do you mean* *To dote thus on such luggage? Let't alone* *And do the murder first!* **or** *If he awake,* *From toe to crown he'll fill our skins with pinches,* *Make us strange stuff.*	This scene confirms for the audience Prospero's view that Caliban is 'A devil, a born devil, on whose nature / Nurture can never stick'. Nevertheless he seems more worthy of respect than the two drunken fools whose concern for mere 'luggage' will, he knows, defeat his project to kill Prospero and bring them real suffering.

Focus on theme

Mark brief quotations in your extracts using a different coloured highlighter for each of the themes shown below. Add your own quotations and annotations for these and for other themes you think are important.

Power and punishment

Points	Quotations	Personal responses
Extract 1 Stephano and Trinculo are drunk and ridiculous, but Caliban, having tasted their 'celestial liquor', sees Stephano as his saviour because he seems brave. We have seen that those of noble birth are not to be trusted – now we see a different style of lord; one of the common men.	*Stephano: Drink, servant-monster, when I bid thee!* *Caliban: Let me lick thy shoe; I'll not serve **him**. He is not valiant.*	The audience of Shakespeare's time will have recognised that the presence of two drunken Englishmen on the island develops the theme of power in terms of exploration and conquest. Sailors in Shakespeare's time did arrive in foreign lands and they ignored the rights of the natives, represented by Caliban.
Stephano is physical in his threats, and hits Trinculo when fooled by invisible Ariel.	*Stephano: If you prove a mutineer – the next tree!* **or** *Stephano: Trinculo, if you trouble him any more in's tale, by this hand, I will supplant some of your teeth.* *Caliban: Beat him enough. After a little time, I'll beat him too.*	Neither Stephano nor Trinculo has any idea how to exercise power responsibly. The audience would enjoy the knockabout humour that the magic creates.
Caliban hates Prospero violently and resents what he sees as Prospero's theft of the island from its rightful owner, himself, but admires Stephano and is ready to serve him.	*Caliban: I am subject to a tyrant, a sorcerer* *...they all do hate him* *As rootedly as I.* *Stephano: ...his daughter and I will be king and queen – save our graces! – and Trinculo and thyself shall be viceroys.*	Caliban's claim that Prospero's servants obey him only out of fear of his magic power has some truth in it. Although they are very different, we notice some similarities between Stephano and Prospero: they both use trees for punishment.
Extract 2 Ariel does not mention the conspiracy because he is wary of his master's temper. Prospero realises that Caliban's evil nature is beyond his control, but knows that his magical power can make the conspirators harmless.	*Ariel: I thought to have told thee of it – but I feared* *Lest I might anger thee.* *Prospero: A devil, a born devil, on whose nature* *Nurture can never stick.* *...Sir, I am vexed;* *Bear with my weakness: my old brain is troubled.*	There are limits to Prospero's power over others – he can do nothing to change Caliban. There are also times when he does not have full control over his own feelings, and we see his struggle with his 'vexed' soul. Seeing that struggle makes us respect him more as a ruler. To have your enemies at your mercy, but to forgive them shows the greatest power, which is self-control.
The more Stephano is praised as a king in his showy garments, the more ridiculous he seems, squabbling over what Caliban rightly calls 'mere luggage' instead of doing 'good mischief' by killing Prospero.	*Caliban: Do that good mischief which may make this island* *Thine own for ever, and I, thy Caliban,* *For aye thy foot-licker.* *Trinculo: O King Stephano! O peer! O worthy Stephano! Look what wardrobe here is for thee!*	Stephano and Trinculo are not the serious plotters in the play, and their punishments, such as being in the 'filthy-mantled pool' are amusing rather than terrifying.
Caliban knows that Prospero will punish them painfully, and he does. The mood changes when Prospero realises that his enemies are all in his power, and keeps Ariel from his freedom only because he needs some final magical services.	*Caliban: From toe to crown he'll fill our skins with pinches,* *Prospero: Go, charge my goblins that they grind their joints...* *At this hour* *Lies at my mercy all mine enemies.* *Thou / Shalt have the air at freedom. For a little* *Follow, and do me service.*	In the first extract Prospero had promised to 'plague them all to roaring' and he does exactly that. The audience know that his real targets are the traitorous nobles, not the common people, however foolish they may be. It may be no accident that one of the hounds is called Tyrant, given that the play has in part been about the power of a ruler.

Focus on theme

Mark brief quotations in your extracts using a different coloured highlighter for each of the themes shown below. Add your own quotations and annotations for these and for other themes you think are important.

Island magic and illusion

Points	Quotations	Personal responses
Extract 1 Stephano does not realise that he has survived the shipwreck only through Prospero's magic.	*Stephano: For my part the sea cannot drown me* *Trinculo: half a fish and half a monster*	The drunken pair think that Caliban is the product of strange magic, but his strangeness is real. One illusion, caused by drink, is Caliban's belief that Stephano is a noble lord.
Ariel is the invisible 'picture of Nobody!', when he interrupts Caliban, but Caliban as a native inhabitant, is used to such magical 'noises, sounds and sweet airs, that give delight and hurt not'. Caliban is aware of the beauty of this island dream world, and has the language to convey this beauty. Caliban's description is so powerful that we are reminded by Shakespeare that all theatre is a kind of illusion.	*Caliban: Be not afeard; the isle is full of noises,* *Sounds and sweet airs, that give delight and hurt not.* *Sometimes a thousand twangling instruments* *Will hum about mine ears…* *… when I waked,* *I cried to dream again.*	The audience, unlike the characters, know exactly what has happened through Prospero's magic. These low-life characters and their conspiracy are a comic parallel for the real conspiracy happening on the island. Ariel's invisible interruption is magic that is designed to create 'slapstick' comedy to make the audience laugh.
Extract 2 We never expected the conspiracy to be allowed to succeed, but forgetting about it gives Prospero a human touch.	*Prospero: I had forgot the foul conspiracy* *Of the beast Caliban and his confederates* **or** *… my old brain is troubled*	This seems surprisingly forgetful from the Gandalf of his day who was so clever, but it does show us the fallible side of a man who is getting old.
When Prospero is talking to Ferdinand and Miranda, there is a sense of things passing from an older generation to a younger, innocent one. The great magician knows that his magic has nearly done its work.	*Our revels now are ended. These our actors,* *As I foretold you, were all spirits – and* *Are melted into air, into thin air:* *…this insubstantial pageant…* **or** *We are such stuff as dreams are made on…*	Prospero describes not only the pageant, but the play itself and the magical illusion that is theatre. This speech is full of references to the theatre and 'I the great globe itself' is an image that would not have been missed, since Shakespeare's company performed at the Globe Theatre.
Prospero needs Ariel as his magical 'enforcer', able to deal with the annoying but not very significant 'conspiracy' of a couple of drunkards. He knows how easy it will be to distract them with 'trumpery'. Power itself is an illusion in some senses – Prospero no longer wants the power that his magic has enabled him to regain.	*Ariel: I left them* *I' the filthy-mantled pool beyond your cell,* **or** *Prospero:* *The trumpery in my house, go bring it hither,* *For stale to catch these thieves.* **or** *Prospero: At this hour* *Lies at my mercy all mine enemies.*	Prospero's punishments are fierce, but we assume temporary, since his mood changes when all his enemies are in his power and he is near releasing Ariel. One more illusion is Stephano's and Trinculo's belief that these are fine clothes, worth squabbling over. Prospero's greatest challenge is to have control over himself, rather than over his enemies. Only when he has such self-control will he be ready to leave the island of illusions and return to the real world that exiled him so long ago.

Focus on language

Highlight the key words in the table below and fill in the blank rows with your own points, quotations and personal responses.

Extract 1: Act 3, Scene 2

Points	Quotations	Personal responses
Stephano is starting to behave like a master, treating Caliban like his servant.	Stephano: My man-monster or Drink, servant-monster, when I bid thee!	By using 'my' and 'when I bid thee' Stephano shows he thinks of Caliban as someone he can command. This shows the audience how having power can go to people's heads. They can start behaving badly and begin treating others like slaves.
Stephano begins to sound like a king as he becomes used to Caliban obeying him.	Stephano: Monsieur Monster or thou shalt be my lieutenant	English kings often spoke in French, so calling Caliban 'Monsieur' makes Stephano sound like a king. He gives Caliban the post of lieutenant, like a king giving out honours. In this extract Stephano becomes more and more like a king in the way he behaves, showing that he is enjoying being in charge. This links to the second extract when they play at dressing up as royalty.
Caliban starts to treat Stephano as if he were his master.	Caliban: I thank my noble lord. or Let me lick thy shoe…	Caliban wants to show Stephano he is obeying him by using polite language like 'noble lord' and showing he will do anything for him, even lick his shoe. Caliban was desperate to escape from Prospero's power but the language he uses shows he is prepared to be ruled by another master, Stephano, who will treat him badly. Caliban demeans himself in the language he uses.
Caliban shows he is sensitive to the beauty of the island's magic.	Caliban: Sounds and sweet airs, that give delight and hurt not. or I cried to dream again.	Caliban shows he likes the magical music by using the words 'delight' and 'sweet'. While Stephano and Trinculo are mainly interested in drinking, Caliban shows he is superior to them because he can appreciate beautiful music and likes the wonderful dreams he has on the island.
Trinculo thinks Caliban's behaviour in worshipping Stephano is foolish.	Trinculo: 'Lord' quoth he? That a monster should be such a natural!	Trinculo calls Caliban a 'natural', meaning foolishly innocent, showing he thinks Caliban can't see that Stephano is not worth worshipping. Trinculo shows he is aware that Caliban's worship of Stephano is ridiculous as Stephano is not worthy of it. Trinculo seems more able to see the situation for what it is. By the second extract he seems to have accepted things and tries on the royal clothes like Stephano.
Caliban's hatred of Prospero is clear from the language he uses.	Caliban:…knock a nail into his head. or Batter his skull…	Caliban uses words like 'batter' to show how violently he wants to attack Prospero. The violence of Caliban's language emphasises the evil of their plot. Rather than just overthrowing Prospero, Caliban wants him killed as painfully as possible.

Focus on language

Highlight the key words in the table below and fill in the blank rows with your own points, quotations and personal responses.

Extract 2: Act 4, Scene 1, lines 139 to 262

Points	Quotations	Personal responses
Prospero describes the way the world will end just like the magic pageant he has created.	Prospero: ...our little life / Is rounded with a sleep. / **or** / Leave not a rack behind.	Everyone's life is small when compared with the history of the world, 'the great globe'. Prospero's speech shows that everything is temporary and will fade. Earthly power won't last and so Antonio and Sebastian's plot to kill King Alonso and Caliban's plot to kill Prospero are both made to seem small and petty.
The foolish behaviour of the drunken Caliban, Stephano and Trinculo is made clear in Ariel's description of them.	Ariel: ...they smote the air / For breathing in their faces... / **or** / ...beat the ground / For kissing of their feet...	Ariel says they were so drunk they were trying to attack the wind for blowing on them and the ground for touching their feet. The language in Ariel's description shows them to be foolish and drunk so the audience realise that they will not be suitable to rule the island.
Prospero shows how upset and angry he feels that Caliban seems to have learned nothing from the way Prospero has tried to care for him.	Prospero: ...on whose nature / Nurture can never stick... / **or** / ...on whom my pains, / Humanely taken, all, all lost, quite lost...	Prospero feels that Caliban's nature is evil and that nurture (care and education) is wasted on him. The bitter words Prospero uses show the audience his anger and disappointment that his efforts to civilise Caliban through caring for him and educating him have failed. Caliban's nature proved too strong; he tried to rape Miranda and wants to kill Prospero as painfully as possible.
Stephano and Trinculo are upset that they have lost their drink in the muddy pool.	Stephano: ...disgrace and dishonour in that ... infinite loss	Disgrace and dishonour are words used for serious events, not just for losing a bottle. These words show the audience that Stephano and Trinculo are unfit to rule the island because they are more worried about their drink than anything else.
Caliban cleverly uses words to persuade Stephano and Trinculo to concentrate on the murder plan.	Caliban: Do that good mischief which may make this island / Thine own for ever... / **or** / ...the prize I'll bring thee to...	Caliban calls the mischief 'good' to try to hide the fact that it is murder he is talking about. He encourages Stephano by reminding him that he will have the island for ever. The audience see how Caliban keeps trying to encourage Stephano and Trinculo to do the murder.
Caliban's words show he knows they are wasting time by playing with the clothes.	Caliban: ...What do you mean / To dote thus on such luggage? ... / **or** / It is but trash.	Caliban can't believe they are wasting time on worthless clothes ('luggage') which they seem to be obsessed by ('dote thus on'). Ariel's trick to distract them with royal clothes shows the audience their foolishness: they are more interested in the gaudy clothes than in carrying out the murder.
The punishments Prospero orders for them are sharp.	Prospero: grind their joints / With dry convulsions; shorten up their sinews...	The words Prospero uses for his punishments are harsh sounding but not violent in the way Caliban's words were in the first extract. The words show the audience that the punishments Prospero orders are painful, but not vicious murder like Caliban is planning.

Focus on performance

Highlight the key words in the table below and fill in the blank rows with your own points, quotations and personal responses.

Extract 1: Act 3, Scene 2

Points	Quotations	Personal responses
Caliban does have a vicious and cruel nature which is shown by the brutal way he tells Stephano how to kill Prospero.	Caliban: ...knock a nail into his head. or Batter his skull, or paunch him with a stake, Or cut his wezand with thy knife.	The actor playing Caliban has to show that he is capable of being savage and cruel. He should growl the lines and show with his hands how Prospero should be killed.
His reaction to Trinculo's taunts is equally savage – he wants him bitten to death and to help Stephano beat him. He has suffered physical punishment at Prospero's hand and thinks this is how humans behave.	Caliban: ...Bite him to death,... or Beat him enough. After a little time, I'll beat him too.	Caliban is not frightened of Trinculo and he should show this by pushing his face close to Trinculo's as if he is ready to fight him.
Caliban can see the beauty of the island because he loves it – it is his home.	Caliban: ...the isle is full of noises, Sounds and sweet airs, that give delight and hurt not. or ...a thousand twangling instruments Will hum about mine ears...	When Caliban speaks these lines he should use a gentle tone of voice to show the audience that he loves his island. As he starts to speak he should slowly rise from the ground until he is standing upright, like a man, for the end of the speech to show that he does have a civilised side to his nature.
The actor has to show the audience that Caliban does have a sensitive side to his nature – just like humans, he has the capacity to dream and understands that dreams can release him from the misery of his life as Prospero's slave.	Caliban: ...in dreaming, The clouds methought would open and show riches Ready to drop on me – that when I waked, I cried to dream again.	This is a very different Caliban from the one we saw at the start of the play and of this scene. He should move to the front of the stage and talk directly to the audience to show that he has for a moment forgotten the other characters. For a short time the audience feels some sympathy for him.
He also has to show that he is happy to serve a drunken fool like Stephano, by looking at him in an adoring way.	Caliban: How does thy honour? Let me lick thy shoe... or I thank my noble lord. or Thou shalt be lord of it, and I'll serve thee.	This subservience is not amusing because the audience knows that Stephano is not noble. It is sad to see Caliban grovelling and simpering at Stephano's feet.
Ariel's mischief-making provides the comedy in this scene. To make this scene effective Caliban and Stephano should immediately look at Trinculo when they hear Ariel's words.	Ariel: Thou liest. or Thou liest: thou canst not.	The actor playing Ariel should show that he finds the antics of the drunken trio amusing by laughing at them once they start arguing.
It does not take long for Stephano to become a bully. Now that he is king he threatens his friend with severe punishments, including death, for the smallest offence. His view of kingship is not a very pleasant one.	Stephano: Drink, servant-monster, when I bid thee! or For my part the sea cannot drown me.... or If you prove a mutineer – the next tree! or ...by this hand, I will supplant some of your teeth.	The actor playing Stephano needs to show how arrogant he has become since Caliban began to worship him and how much he enjoys having power over his friend, Trinculo. He should swagger about the stage with his head held high to show that he feels he is more important than the others.

Focus on performance

Highlight the key words in the table below and fill in the blank rows with your own points, quotations and personal responses.

Extract 2: Act 4, Scene 1, lines 139 to 262

Points	Quotations	Personal responses
The actor playing Prospero must show how agitated he is about Caliban's plot to kill him. He should look angry and distracted as he thinks about the plot. When he speaks the aside he could thump his staff on the ground to show how angry he is.	Prospero: ...that foul conspiracy of the beast Caliban... or ...still my beating mind.	Caliban's plot to kill Prospero and make Stephano king mirrors what Prospero's brother did to him when he was Duke of Milan. Prospero is angry that once again a disloyal subject has threatened his life.
Even Miranda is worried about Prospero as she has never seen him in this mood before. The actor playing Miranda should show her surprise by emphasising the words 'so distempered'.	Ferdinand: ...Your father's in some passion That works him strongly. Miranda: ...touched with anger, so distempered.	This is a sign that the pressure of bringing all the elements of his plan together is taking its toll on him. It also helps build the dramatic tension for the audience because we know that Caliban and the two sailors are in for an unpleasant shock when they come to kill Prospero.
The actor playing Ariel should speak in a subdued voice when confessing his/her reluctance to tell Prospero about Caliban to show that s/he is still afraid of Prospero's temper. When making entrances and exits Ariel should speak very quickly to show how eager s/he is to do what Prospero wants.	Ariel: Thy thoughts I cleave to. What's thy pleasure? or ...I feared Lest I might anger thee. or I go, I go.	Ariel is the perfect servant – he does as he is told as he knows that it would be a mistake to make his master angry with him. Ariel has to show how keen he is to please his master, and knows that the subject of Caliban always makes Prospero angry.
The actor playing Caliban should show his disappointment by turning his back on the two men when they ignore his pleas to 'let't alone', which is very different from his behaviour in the first extract.	Caliban: Let't alone, thou fool! It is but trash. or What do you mean To dote thus on such luggage? or I will have none on't!	Caliban realises that Stephano is not the noble master he thought he was and the plot to kill Prospero has failed. The words 'trash' and 'luggage' used to describe the clothes are also what Stephano has become in Caliban's eyes.
The actors playing Trinculo and Stephano should dress themselves in as many clothes as they can so they end up looking ridiculous.	Trinculo: ...And this Stephano: ...Ay, and this	The characters' reactions to the pile of clothes show the audience how foolish they are. Their greed for a pile of gaudy clothes is both sad and pitiful and shows how unfit they are to be rulers of anything – certainly not the island.
Prospero should show that he is in complete control of the situation by issuing his orders to Ariel in a commanding and stern voice. He should stand in the centre of the stage to show that he is in charge of the situation.	Prospero: Let them be hunted or At my mercy or All my labours or or Do me service	The use of the pronouns 'my'/'me' shows how confident Prospero is that he has routed the plot to kill him and that his great plan to punish his enemies has been successful.

Character response grid (PEEE)

Think about the statements in the first column, and fill in your response in the appropriate column, giving the evidence from the set extracts, then explaining and exploring your thinking. The first line has been completed for you as an example.

Character response grid

Statement	Response	Y/N	Evidence	Explanation	Exploration
Prospero's use of power is not much better than Stephano's	Definitely		*Stephano: The poor monster's my subject...* *Stephano: Monster, I will kill this man; his daughter and I will be king and queen – save our graces!* *Prospero: ...grind their joints... Lies at my mercy all my enemies.*	Stephano is still drunk and loves being treated like a ruler. It would be hard to appear less like a king than Stephano does at this point. Prospero, although cruel, can be forgiving.	Stephano has no understanding of the responsibilities of power. The prospect of killing Prospero does not bother him, so the contrast with Prospero, who can give up his power, is clear.
	Yes, on balance				
	Not really				
	No way	Yes			
Caliban despises Trinculo and tries to break his friendship with Stephano because he is jealous of him	Definitely				
	Yes, on balance				
	Not really				
	No way				
Trinculo has more sense than Stephano in both scenes	Definitely				
	Yes, on balance				
	Not really				
	No way				
The audience has more sympathy with Caliban than with the two drunkards	Definitely				
	Yes, on balance				
	Not really				
	No way				
Caliban's descriptions of Prospero as a tyrant are justified	Definitely				
	Yes, on balance				
	Not really				
	No way				
Stephano and Trinculo are shown as good friends throughout these extracts	Definitely				
	Yes, on balance				
	Not really				
	No way				

The Key Stage 3 Shakespeare test

How to approach the test

Remember that:

- The Shakespeare test accounts for 18 out of the 50 marks for reading. You gain marks by showing that you understand and have responded to *The Tempest*.
- The way you write matters, because it enables you to make your points effectively, but you will not be judged on how well you write. No marks are given (or taken off) for spelling or expression.
- The extracts you will be expected to write about will be printed in the test paper. Don't make the mistake of writing about all of the set scenes – concentrate on the two extracts you are given.
- PQR (**P**oint, **Q**uotation, **R**esponse) is better than PEE because it includes your personal reaction to the play.
- Short quotations are better than long ones because they save you time in the test.

Top tips for the test

- Keep in mind performances of the play that you have seen, in the theatre or on video.
- Remember what it was like acting out the set scenes with other people.
- Make sure that you are familiar with the layout and style of questions by looking at tests from previous years.
- Read the question aloud in your head two or three times until you realise what it is really asking you to do, then underline or highlight the key words in the question.
- Don't ever just tell the story – answer the question.
- Time spent on planning is time well spent. Practise doing a plan in five minutes so that in the real test you can create a plan quickly and effectively.
- Plan so that your main points are in a sensible order that responds to the question.
- Provide evidence in quotation or refer to what happens and is said to support your points. (Don't waste time copying out long quotations.)
- Make sure that your conclusion relates back to the question.
- Leave time (but not too much) at the end of the test to read through what you have written.

What will the questions be on?

The question on *The Tempest* should be on **one** of the areas (or 'big ideas') below, although you usually need to refer to the other areas as part of your answer:

- why **characters** behave as they do in the extracts given
- the impact of the **language** used in the extracts
- **ideas**, **themes** and **issues** that are relevant to the extracts
- how these extracts might be **performed** in the theatre.

Key Stage 3 marking

How will my answer be marked?

The emphasis in marking will depend on the focus of the question, but generally answers are awarded level 5 or above if they:

- include comment on both of the extracts given on the paper
- reveal some understanding of character and dramatic action
- refer to the main features of the language in the extracts and the effect this language might have
- show some awareness of how an audience might respond
- illustrate points made, by picking out words or phrases from the text as evidence
- include your personal response to specific aspects of the extracts.

Answers on Shakespeare are allocated to mark bands. The characteristics of different mark bands for a question on **language** are set out below.

	General characteristics	**What will that look like to an examiner?**
1	Mainly retelling the story with a few simple facts and opinions about the focus of the question.	General comments that show only limited understanding of the extracts or the question, e.g. *Caliban worships both the two drunkards.* The two extracts are not treated equally, and there may be much storytelling.
2	Some response to the question. Some broad references to the way character(s) speak or behave.	Some comment on what characters do and say, e.g. *Caliban treats Stephano like a king, but does not like Trinculo.* The two extracts may not be treated equally and simple references may not be linked with comments. There may be some reference to some words or phrases such as 'the isle is full of noises'.
3	Shows general understanding of characters' feelings and of the way language reveals character and refers to textual evidence.	Secure general understanding of the impression an audience might have of characters and what their language shows about how they develop, e.g. *Caliban's language of 'lord', 'noble lord' shows that he treats Stephano like a king, but he despises Trinculo, calls him a 'pied ninny' and wants him beaten.* Points are generally illustrated by relevant references to the text, but comments are likely to be repeated rather than developed. Limited comment on the effects of language, but does include comments on both extracts.
4	Shows awareness of characters' feelings and how this is shown through language and its effects.	May provide some discussion of how the language and behaviour of characters creates the audience's impressions of them, e.g. *When Prospero says 'Sir I am vexed; Bear with my weakness' his tone of voice and choice of words show that he is thinking about what to do once he has power over all his enemies.* Relevant references from both extracts will be included and there should be clear understanding of the broader context of the play. Explicit comments on the effects of characters' uses of language in both extracts would be expected.
5	Clear focus on the question asked, with understanding of the way language is used and of its effects. Well-chosen references to the text justify comments as part of an overall argument. Shows consciousness of how Shakespeare might have wanted his characters to speak and behave.	A relevant and focused answer which engages confidently with both extracts. Aspects of the text will be explored, not just explained, in ways that show a wider understanding of the play's development, e.g. *When Prospero says 'Sir I am vexed; Bear with my weakness' his tone of voice and choice of words show the tensions in him as a vulnerable man not just as an all-powerful magician.* The selection of well-chosen references builds into a sustained argument which includes comment on the dramatic effect of the language used.
6	Appreciation of the features and effects of language, linked with coherent analysis of characters' actions and attitudes. Comments and precisely selected references to the text are integrated into well-developed argument.	A focused and developed analysis of the impression created by a character through language and action on stage. The answer engages analytically with both extracts, showing insight into the less obvious aspects of the text and an ability to contextualise ideas, e.g. *When Prospero says 'Sir I am vexed; Bear with my weakness' his tone of voice and choice of words show the tensions in him as a man who has power over others through his magic but is struggling to convince himself that the rarer action is in virtue than in vengeance.* Appreciation of the features and effects of language is well supported by integrated references. There may be recognition of the possibility of different interpretations of the text.

Sample questions

Thinking about the question: an example

> I must write in detail about Caliban, Stephano and Trinculo, and bring out the differences between Caliban and the others.

> I'll base my answer very firmly on the words in a few short quotations and avoid general comments.

How do Stephano, Trinculo and Caliban respond to the magic of the island in these two extracts?

> I must remember that the focus of the question is the **magic** of the island.

> I need to refer to **both** of the two extracts as equally as I can.

Sample questions

Themes
- Power and punishment
- Island magic and illusion

- What do these two extracts add to an audience's understanding of the theme of power and punishment?
- How do Stephano, Trinculo and Caliban respond to the magic of the island in these two extracts?

Character
- What do these two extracts show about differences and similarities between Stephano and Trinculo?
- What impressions of Caliban are created through what he says and does in these two extracts?
- How does Caliban's view of Stephano and Trinculo change between these two extracts?

Language
- How does Caliban's language in these two extracts show different aspects of his character?
- Explain how language is used in these two extracts to express different characters' feelings about the island.
- In these two extracts how does Caliban use language to try to persuade Stephano and Trinculo to overthrow Prospero?

Performance
- How would you advise the actor playing Caliban to show his changing attitudes to Stephano and Trinculo?
- What advice might the director of a school performance give to the actors playing Stephano, Trinculo and Caliban on how to respond to each other in these two extracts?

Sample answer with examiner's comments

What do these two extracts show an audience about having power over others?

General understanding of what the characters feel about their position on the island

Both extracts are about having power over others, and they show an audience what it means to use power wisely. Prospero does eventually use his power wisely, though he sometimes uses his power cruelly. Being a ruler like a king in Shakespeare's time meant having power and using servants to do what you want such as punishing enemies. Stephano wants to become the King of the island by killing Prospero and marrying his daughter, but he is a drunkard who could not use power.

Stephano is a servant and is not used to having any power, but he behaves as the ruler of Caliban and Trinculo by using drink. Caliban accepts Stephano as his master as he has given him drink. Caliban wants Stephano to kill Prospero and to become King of the island. But the audience can see how foolish the idea of drunk Stephano as 'king' of the island is.

Some use of language to illustrate points made

Stephano tries to show his power through his language by giving orders: 'Tell not me.' He calls Caliban 'servant' and 'monster'. He enjoys having power and demands that Caliban 'kneel' to him. Caliban is used to being a servant and he calls Stephano 'valiant master', saying he will 'lick thy shoe'.

Some discussion of Stephano's attitude to kingship. This is supported by Caliban's response

Here the reference to language builds up an awareness of the nature of power by using well-chosen quotes

Trinculo is jealous of Caliban and when Ariel pretends to be Trinculo and begins to make rude comments, Caliban asks Stephano to 'bite him' because he thinks having power means punishing people. Stephano thinks power is giving out physical punishments, so he threatens to hang Trinculo from 'the next tree'. This reminds the audience of Prospero's threats to Ariel. The audience can see that Prospero and Stephano are not all that different, since physical power is important to both of them in the extracts.

Caliban wants to use power very violently against Prospero: 'Batter his skull', 'cut his wezand'. Stephano is ready to kill for his 'honour' but the scene shows us what a terrible ruler Stephano would be and that he does not have any deeper understanding of honour than Caliban.

How the effects of language create parody

In extract two Prospero remembers the conspiracy. Ariel punishes the bad conspirators by leading them into the 'filthy-mantled pool'. Prospero does not show mercy but he doesn't want to kill them, showing that he uses power better than Stephano. 'I will plague them'. The dressing-up clothes show that Stephano and Trinculo would not use power at all wisely because they just want to look good in the 'trash' clothes. Caliban is disgusted with them when he says 'such luggage'. Caliban wants them to kill Prospero quickly because he fears more punishment. Stephano has no sense of what a true ruler would do, and he is distracted by the clothes 'trumpery'. This is a comic scene but it is not just comic – Shakespeare could also be saying that some rulers could be more interested in dressing up than in ruling well.

Discussion about kingship in its historical context to give personal response

Discussion about the characters' contrasting attitudes

Finally the audience see how Prospero has the magical power to hunt down his enemies. Prospero has all his enemies at his mercy, not just Stephano and Trinculo. He could have 'bloody thoughts' of killing like Stephano, but instead he chooses to hurt them with 'cramps' and 'convulsions' rather than kill them. In this scene, Prospero seems to think rulers must make sure that wrongdoers get the punishments they deserve.

Clear focus on how the effects of language show different attitudes

Planning a character answer

Spend at least five minutes on planning in the test.

> ## How does Caliban's view of Stephano and Trinculo change between these two extracts?

Read and re-read the question very carefully, and underline or highlight the key words.

I'll use the planning approach that suits me, e.g. pattern notes, diagram, list of points and quotations.

Write about both the test extracts given with the focus on how Caliban's view changes between the two extracts.

My opening points will be:
- Caliban begins by worshipping them in extract 1 and ends by despising them in extract 2.
- He is drunk in extract 1 but is sober in 2.

I need a powerful opening based closely on the text, such as Stephano saying that his man-monster 'hath drowned his tongue in sack'. No wonder Caliban is fooled by them.

Language is my vital evidence:
Thy honour and *my noble lord* give way to anger in extract 2 – *thou fool* and finally *I will have none on't.*

His view of Trinculo does not change as much as that of Stephano – he is jealous and hates Trinculo from the start.

I will develop these points:
Caliban thinks at first that they can remove Prospero, and admires their magic bottle. He becomes frustrated when in extract 2 they are diverted by 'trash' from his desire to murder Prospero.

I must keep quotations or references very brief – two words are better than two lines.

Finally
I will summarise by saying that although Caliban is not human, we sympathise more with him than with Stephano and Trinculo as his drunkenness wears off and his view of them becomes clearer.

I'll leave time at the end to look back and check that I answered the question fully.

REMEMBER Marking 300 similar answers does get boring, so examiners appreciate a personal voice in an answer which does not just state the obvious.

Planning a theme answer

Spend at least five minutes on planning in the test.

> **What do these two extracts add to an audience's understanding of the theme of power and punishment?**

In the first few minutes, read and re-read the question **very** carefully, and underline or highlight the key words.

The focus is on the ideas of power and punishment, not just on what the characters say or do.

I must mention **both** extracts, and keep in mind that themes are conveyed through words and through actions on stage.

I must have a powerful opening point and an effective way of ending and keep quotations or references very brief.

My opening points will be:
- Extract 1 and extract 2 show that Stephano's physical power differs from Prospero's magical power.
- Both feature punishment.
- Prospero has the power to give up power over others.

Language is very important. I must say **how** and **why** particular words like *beat* contribute to exploring the theme.

I will develop these points by writing about the language about power used in both extracts:
- by Caliban about Prospero, Stephano and Trinculo
- by Ariel about Prospero
- by Prospero about control and self-control.

I must say **how** Prospero expresses his thoughts about power over others and over himself, and **why** this is so important.

I will extend these points by writing about what happens on stage in the two extracts:
- Stephano beats Trinculo and plans murder.
- Prospero has the conspirators punished by being in the *filthy mantled pool* but humiliates rather than harms them.

I would comment on **how** characters behave and **why** this is important to the theme.

My conclusion would:
Refer back to the title with comments on how our view of power and control differs in the two extracts. The first features low-level violence and the second focuses more on the magical power of Prospero who has more self-control, but still punishes his enemies.

Have I kept the title in mind throughout?

Planning a language answer

Spend at least five minutes on planning in the test.

> **How does Caliban's language in these two extracts show different aspects of his character?**

Read and re-read the question **very** carefully, and underline or highlight the key words.

> The focus is on language. I must remember to make everything I write based on the words Caliban says. I must mention **both** extracts, and keep in mind that the quotes must be related to Caliban's character.

My key points will be:
- The language Caliban uses in these extracts is very varied.
- Different sides of his character are shown to the audience by what he says.

> I must have a powerful opening point and an effective way of ending and keep quotations or references very brief.

I will write about how Caliban's words show different feelings about Stephano and Trinculo and how the feelings change between the two extracts:
- he shows he idolises Stephano and wants to be ruled
- he has contempt for Trinculo
- at the end of the second extract he has lost patience with them.

> Quotes like 'lick thy feet' show he idolises Stephano, 'thou fool' how he feels about Trinculo and 'dote on such luggage' shows he has lost faith in them in extract 2.

Next I will show how his words reveal a range of feelings from hatred to an enjoyment of music and beauty:
- he shows his hatred through the cruelty of his plans
- how the beauty of the island affects him.

> I will use a quote like 'with a log batter his skull' to show how his character is full of hatred and evil.

> The quote 'give delight' could be used to show he is also a sensitive person who can appreciate beauty.

I will then show how Caliban is clever and cunning:
- he uses words cleverly to tempt Stephano
- he cleverly puts in reminders that they must kill Prospero
- the way he describes the murder plan shows cunning.

> 'she will become thy bed' shows cunning, 'when Prospero is destroyed' is a reminder of his plan for Prospero.

My conclusion would:
Refer back to the title and say that Caliban's words in the extracts show him to be a more complex character than he seems when the audience first sees him.

> Have I kept the focus on Caliban's language throughout?

Planning a performance answer

Spend at least five minutes on planning in the test.

> **What advice might the director of a school performance give to the actors playing Stephano, Trinculo and Caliban on how to respond to each other in these two extracts?**

In the first few minutes, read and re-read the question **very** carefully, and underline or highlight the key words.

The focus is on **why** the actors should speak and act on stage in particular ways to help the audience understand their feelings.

I must mention **both** extracts, and keep in mind that this a performance, on a stage like The Globe, not just a book to be read.

My key points will be how to show:
- these characters' attitudes to each other
- changes in mood during the extracts
- how their performances differ in the two extracts
- how to provoke an audience reaction.

I must have a powerful opening point and an effective way of ending and keep quotations or references very brief.

My advice on how to say words will include:
- Stephano and Trinculo have common accents to make the idea of them as rulers funnier.
- Caliban speaks differently from the others, but at times he speaks beautifully when describing the island.

Language is very important. I must say **how** to speak particular words and explain **why** their effect is significant.

My advice on how to act on stage will be:
- How to show the relationship through facial expressions, gestures, position on stage and movement (I needn't bother about costumes or props).
- How to convey on stage the difference in Caliban's attitude to the others in the two extracts: he moves from drunken admiration to sober contempt.
- How to make the audience laugh.

I would comment on **why** and **how** Trinculo and Caliban jostle for Stephano's attention.

I must say **why** and **how** characters should show their feelings on stage and how their behaviour on stage differs in the two extracts.

My conclusion would:
Refer to the title with comments on the intended effect of language and give a sense of how the audience might respond to the characters **because of** the actions and gestures I have suggested.

Have I kept the title in mind throughout?